D0768825

Ancient Egyptian Civilization

Pyramids
of Ancient Egypt

By Christopher Forest

Consultant:
Jennifer Houser Wegner, PhD
Associate Curator, Egyptian Section
Penn Museum, Pennsylvania

CAPSTONE PRESS
a capstone imprint

Fact Finder Books are published by Capstone Press,
1710 Roe Crest Drive, North Mankato, Minnesota 56003
www.capstonepub.com

 Books published by Capstone Press are manufactured with paper
containing at least 10 percent post-consumer waste.

Library of Congress Cataloging-in-Publication Data
Forest, Christopher.
Pyramids of ancient Egypt / by Christopher Forest; consultant, Jen
Houser Wegner.
      p. cm. — (Fact finders. Ancient Egyptian civilization)
Includes bibliographical references and index.
 ISBN 978-1-4296-7632-8 (library binding)
 ISBN 978-1-4296-7980-0 (paperback)
 1. Pyramids—Egypt—Juvenile literature. I. Wegner, Jennifer Houser.
II. Title. III. Series.

DT63.F73 2012
932—dc23   2011033541

Editorial Credits
Brenda Haugen, editor; Juliette Peters, series designer; Wanda Winch, photo researcher;
     Laura Manthe, production specialist

Photo Credits
akg-images, 8; Bridgeman Art Library International: Private Collection/Dudley C. Tennant, 11;
Corbis: Werner Forman, 9; Dreamstime: Jgaunion, 7, Onefivenine, 28, Petr Svec, 20; Newscom: AFP/
Khaled Desouki, 5, akg-images/Herve Champollion, 17; Photo Researchers, Inc: Christian Jegou,
14; Shutterstock: artform, hieroglyphs used throughout, Carlos Arguelles, 18, fstockfoto, 22, Mikhail
Dudarev, pyramids (used throughout book), Nestor Noci, 26, Pius Lee, 24, Rafa Irusta, papyrus,
symbols used throughout, R-studio, gold texture used throughout, sculpies, cover (pyramids),
Vladimir Korostyshevskiy, 16; Wood Ronsaville Harlin, Inc.: Rob Wood, 13

Printed in the United States of America in North Mankato, Minnesota.

032012   006665R

TABLE OF CONTENTS

Chapter 1

Uncovering History

Amazing news spread like wildfire from Cairo, Egypt, in November 2008. Outside Cairo at the site of Saqqara, archaeologists made a remarkable find. For more than 20 years, archaeologists had searched the site to learn more about ancient Egypt. They hoped to find evidence of life in ancient Egypt near the pyramid of Teti. Teti had ruled Egypt more than 4,300 years ago during a period called the Sixth Dynasty. Surely the land would hold secrets of the past. And it did.

Deep in the sands, archaeologists unearthed a historic treasure. The remains of a 4,300-year-old pyramid were found buried in the sand. Scientists studied carvings on stone. They soon realized the pyramid had once belonged to Teti's mother, Queen Sesheshet.

archaeologist: a scientist who studies how people lived in the past

dynasty: a period of time during which a country's rulers all come from one family

The pyramid was five stories high—at least it was at one time. Wind and sand had worn away some of the structure. And previous archaeologists had used the site as a dumping ground for sand dug from other sites. The discovery proved that pyramids are not only monuments to the past, they are exciting parts of the future. There is still much to learn as historians continue to uncover the secrets of Egyptian pyramids.

Archaeologists work at Saqqara in 2008.

Chapter 2

Marvels of Creation

Pyramids may seem like huge old buildings in the desert. In reality, they are amazing memorials to Egyptian pharaohs who died long ago. Why would a pharaoh need a pyramid? Many ancient Egyptians viewed a pharaoh as a god on Earth. People hoped to honor and remember these kings and their families when they died.

The most famous pyramids were built between 2700 and 1700 BC. These buildings were made of limestone and other rock found in Egypt. There are 35 major pyramids in Egypt's Nile Valley. These pyramids are known for their four sloping sides. Historians believe that the sloping sides may have had a religious purpose. The pyramids were thought of as a ladder by which the dead pharaoh would rise into the sky. The sloped sides, pointing skyward, may have reminded the Egyptians of their sun god, Ra.

Egyptians filled the pyramids with precious jewels, gold, perfume, and statues. They believed the pharaohs used these treasures in the afterlife. Temples were sometimes attached to pyramids. Egyptians may have held pharaohs' funerals at the temples. Followers also worshipped the dead pharaohs in these temples.

the Bent Pyramid

Types of Tombs

Mastabas—burial mounds with tunnels and shafts that led to a burial chamber

Step pyramid—a mastaba that was covered by layers of stone

Cased pyramid—classic pyramid of Egypt that was made of stone encased in limestone

pharaoh: a king of ancient Egypt

afterlife: the life that begins when a person dies

Why Were Pyramids Built?

Ancient Egyptians thought pharaohs were gods, but they knew that these gods would one day die. They believed once a pharaoh died a part of his spirit remained. This spirit, called a ka, followed the pharaoh into the afterlife. The ka helped the pharaoh rule over the dead in the afterlife.

King Tutankhamun's body is prepared for burial.

Most Egyptians believed that preserving a pharaoh's body was necessary for a successful afterlife. First, ancient Egyptians turned the body into a mummy. Then they made preparations to keep the body safe. That's where the pyramids come in. A pyramid served as a final resting place for a pharaoh's body. This tomb protected the pharaoh's ka. It also was a spot for Egyptians to store items they thought pharaohs might need in the afterlife.

Before the Egyptians built pyramids, they buried important people in tombs called mastabas. Mastabas were built above shafts that led to burial chambers. The burial chambers could be as deep as 90 feet (27 meters) below ground. Egyptians decorated these chambers with pictures of daily life. Egyptians buried the bodies of pharaohs and other important people in the chambers. The Egyptians covered the chambers with large mounds of mud-baked brick. Visitors walked into a mastaba through an entrance that led to chambers or long tunnels. Royal mastabas were often replaced by more complex tombs. These are the pyramids that still stand today.

FACT

The Pyramid of King Unas was the first pyramid to have decorations on the inside walls. The decorations were called the Pyramid Texts. Many were magical spells that were supposed to help the king in the afterlife.

inside the Pyramid of King Unas

Pyramid Builders

Imagine a whole town working to build one structure. This is exactly what pyramid construction was like. Pharaohs relied on their own priests and architects to design the structures. Priests chose the location for the structures. Architects planned the pyramid layout.

Ordinary citizens built the pyramid. Historians believe that pharaohs drafted Egyptian villagers to build the pyramids. These villagers often worked as farmers throughout the year. But when the Nile River flooded, harvesting was difficult. So Egyptians left their farms and formed large worker villages. These villages often included 20,000 to 30,000 people who worked together to build pyramids.

Men built most of the pyramids. They cut and hauled stones. Archaeologists have found remains of women at some pyramid sites. These remains suggest that women may have hauled stones as well. Besides builders, the villages also contained cooks, brewers, butchers, and even doctors. Workers may have been paid in food or clothing. However, some historians believe workers were forced to build the pyramids to pay their taxes.

The villagers mainly worked on the pyramids during the summer. Egyptologists believe the villagers formed five large groups that worked in shifts. Each shift was often considered its own community. It took decades for the villagers to build one pyramid.

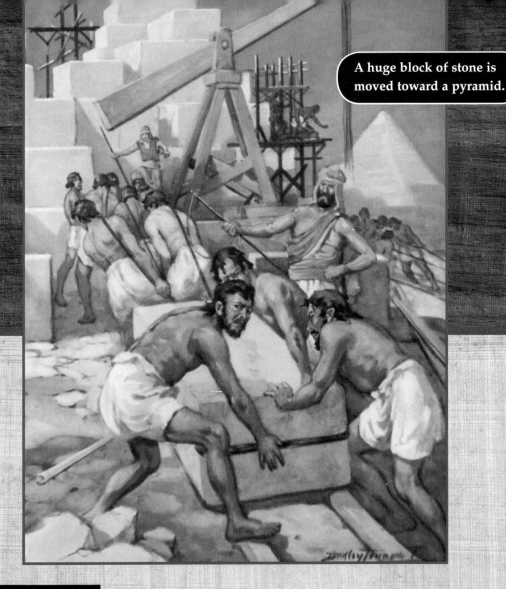

A huge block of stone is moved toward a pyramid.

FACT

Workers left graffiti in the ancient pyramids. They left their own marks behind, often to show which group had built a section of the structure. One famous mark from the Great Pyramid translates into "the Friends of Khufu Gang."

Egyptologist: a person who studies Egypt

graffiti: pictures or words painted on buildings

How Were Pyramids Built?

How long does it take to build one of the wonders of the world? In most cases, one pyramid took more than 10 years to build. And this was no simple task. Chiseling tons of stone and hauling it was hard work. Fighting the heat of the summer and periods of drought took its toll on workers. Pyramid builders risked their lives every day. One false move and a 4,000 pound (1,814 kilogram) boulder could crush workers in seconds.

Pyramid building proved a long and involved process. Determining a location for the pyramid was the first step. Priests were asked to help find a suitable site along the Nile River. The priests may have chosen sites that lined up with stars in the sky. Choosing the right site helped the Egyptians honor their gods. Then architects and engineers laid out a plan worthy of a pharaoh.

Once priests and pharaohs came up with a plan, building began. Workers waited until the Nile flooded to begin work. The floodwaters made hauling materials easier. Men carved granite or limestone blocks from quarries in cities along the river. The workers used copper chisels and saws to carve 3,000 pound (1,361 kg) stones.

quarry: a place where stone or other minerals are dug from the ground

Stone blocks were cut at a quarry and loaded onto a waiting barge.

Workers dragged the blocks, sometimes using wooden sleds, from the quarry to the Nile River. There they were carried up the river on **barges** and then dragged to the base of a pyramid. An average of eight men hauled each block. It took the men about 10 days to lug one block from the quarry to the pyramid site. The largest pyramids required more than 2 million blocks.

barge: a large, flat ship used to transport goods

Workers started by building the base of the pyramid. They polished blocks to make them smooth. Then they carefully fit the blocks together by sliding them into place. Any stones that did not fit together were recut until they fit. The architects designed the base to be a perfect square. A square base helped make the structure look and stand perfectly.

A pharaoh closely watched a pyramid project's progress.

Most historians believe that once the base was complete, builders created a ramp outside of the pyramid. This ramp was made of mud-baked brick. It allowed workers to build levels on top of the base. Egyptians had no cranes or forklifts. So they dragged the blocks up the ramp with ropes and sleds. Builders dragged blocks up this ramp to build the next level. Once the builders completed a level, they made their ramp taller. This way builders could add the next level. Ropes also ran from the base of the pyramid to the top of each level being built. The ropes were used to make sure the pyramid walls lined up properly. Builders continued this way until they fitted the capstone, the final piece, on the pyramid's top.

As soon as the final stones were placed, the workers began the encasing process. During the encasing process, workers placed smooth stones on the outside of the pyramid. The stones helped protect the pyramid from wind and heat. Stones also gave a pyramid a smooth appearance. Builders then took apart any ramps to complete construction.

FACT

Not every pyramid-building project was successful. The Maidum Pyramid of Snefru was completed around 2494 BC. It was a step pyramid. Later builders filled in the steps to make it a true pyramid. No one knows when, but after this change the pyramid collapsed.

Chapter 3

Inside the Pyramids

Each pyramid was built for a different pharaoh, but most had similar design features. Workers usually placed the pyramid entrance in the center of the northern wall. A variety of structures were built around the pyramid. These included tombs for the pharaoh's relatives. Other buildings found at some sites included small memorials and a pharaoh's temple. A path of block connected the temple to the pyramid.

the entrance to the Great Pyramid

Workers didn't just work on the outside of a pyramid. They worked on the inside as well. A tour of a pyramid's interior uncovers many features.

Passages——Right inside the pyramid entrance were long passages. Egyptians used these passages to transport many items. These passages led to a variety of places. Some led to rooms called chambers. The pharaoh's body would be laid in the king's chamber. The passage to that chamber might be up to 150 feet (46 m) long. Other passages led to dead ends. Pyramid builders designed these dead ends to trick potential grave robbers. Starting in the Fifth Dynasty, writings or paintings to protect the pharaohs often lined the pyramid walls.

Pyramid Thieves

Egyptians loved their pharaohs and honored them with pyramids. However, some Egyptians loved the treasures contained in the pyramids as well. The jewels and metals proved tempting to many thieves. The craftiest builders couldn't outsmart grave robbers with fake chambers and false passages. Most pyramids were robbed over time. Many of the treasures were removed from chambers, but looters did not stop there. Some grave robbers unwrapped the bodies of the dead and took jewels from them too.

Chambers—Most pyramids had a variety of chambers. One chamber often served as a burial place for the king. Others were places to hold items used to mummify the pharaoh's body. Some chambers held objects a king might need in the afterlife such as treasures, food, or clothing.

King's chamber—The king's chamber was a pharaoh's final resting place. A **sarcophagus** was placed inside this chamber. Builders constructed the king's chamber as a pyramid was built. In many pyramids, the king's chamber helped support the structure's massive weight.

In most pyramids, the chamber was near the ground level or just below it. Some rose quite high. The king's chamber in the Great Pyramid stood nearly 20 feet (6 m) high. In many pyramids, the king's chamber included walls covered with **hieroglyphs**. The hieroglyphs showed pictures of daily life. They also included spells to help the king make a successful passage to the afterlife.

sarcophagus: a stone coffin; the ancient Egyptians placed inner coffins into a sarcophagus

hieroglyph: a picture or symbol used in the ancient Egyptian system of writing

Shafts—The Great Pyramid is the only pyramid known to have shafts. It contains four shafts. Historians once believed shafts allowed air to flow into the pyramid. However, no one is sure about their use. The shafts don't connect to the outside of the pyramid. So it is possible that the pyramid may have also served the pharaoh. Some historians believe Egyptians felt the dead king's spirit left through a shaft in the Great Pyramid.

Did Pyramids Contain Rigged Traps?

Check out any movie involving the pyramids. You'll see characters avoiding sand that threatens to bury them alive. Or the actors may have to avoid poisonous snakes or crushing boulders. But most pyramids probably did not have such traps or hazards. Instead, workers built false chambers and long corridors leading nowhere inside the pyramids. Workers used these tricks to prevent grave robbers from stealing anything. The fear of getting lost inside a pyramid kept most people from trying to break into one.

Chapter 4

Famous Pyramids

What Was the First Pyramid?

Pyramid of Djoser

Style: step pyramid
Date: 2650 BC
Location: Saqqara
Purpose: tomb of
Pharaoh Djoser

King Djoser was a powerful leader who ruled Egypt during Egypt's Third Dynasty. Djoser extended his country's border to the south. He proved a strong leader who helped to increase Egypt's power. The country grew larger and wealthier through the development of turquoise mines.

FACT

Djoser was buried in his tomb, but no one knows what happened to his body. All that remains of Djoser is a mummified left foot.

Djoser ordered the construction of the first Egyptian pyramid. At first it looked like nothing special. It started as a mastaba that was covered in layers of stone. Then workers decided to create more mastabas on top of the original. When done, the pyramid rose 204 feet (62 m) and had six levels called steps. In some places, workers carved stone so it would look like other materials, including wood. It took 19 years to complete. The workers placed Djoser's burial chamber underground. They also carved a variety of tunnels designed to outsmart grave robbers. These tunnels didn't work. The pyramid and its riches were eventually plundered.

The Father of the Modern Pyramid

Ever wonder who that creepy mummy is in all those scary mummy movies? In most stories he is called Imhotep. Though the mummy onscreen is make-believe, there was a real person named Imhotep. He built the first step pyramid for Djoser. Imhotep helped come up with the plan for pyramid building in Egypt. But he was more than just an architect. He also practiced medicine and studied the stars for the pharaohs. And he was nothing like the mummy movie monsters. His name means "he who comes in peace." Imhotep was also once worshipped as a god.

What Is the Most Famous Pyramid?

The Great Pyramid

Style: cased pyramid
Date: 2585 BC
Location: Giza plateau
Purpose: tomb of
  Pharaoh Khufu

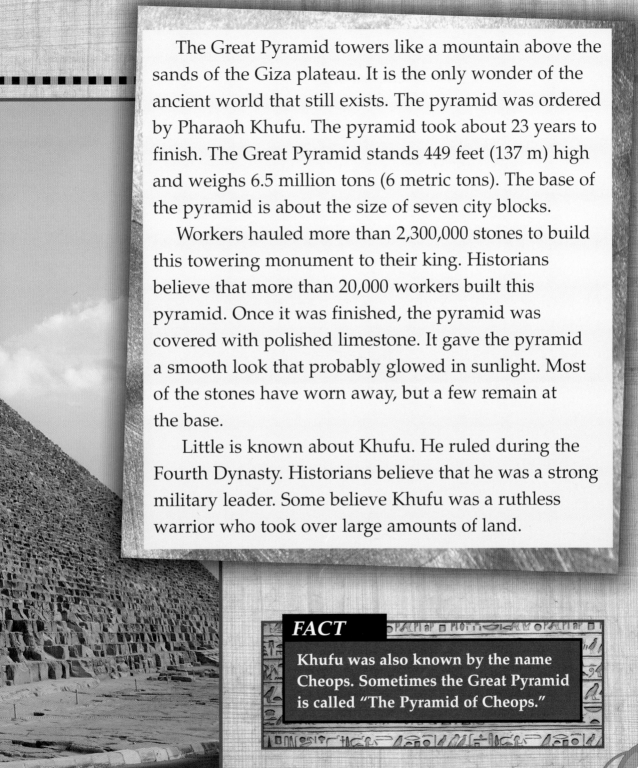

The Great Pyramid towers like a mountain above the sands of the Giza plateau. It is the only wonder of the ancient world that still exists. The pyramid was ordered by Pharaoh Khufu. The pyramid took about 23 years to finish. The Great Pyramid stands 449 feet (137 m) high and weighs 6.5 million tons (6 metric tons). The base of the pyramid is about the size of seven city blocks.

Workers hauled more than 2,300,000 stones to build this towering monument to their king. Historians believe that more than 20,000 workers built this pyramid. Once it was finished, the pyramid was covered with polished limestone. It gave the pyramid a smooth look that probably glowed in sunlight. Most of the stones have worn away, but a few remain at the base.

Little is known about Khufu. He ruled during the Fourth Dynasty. Historians believe that he was a strong military leader. Some believe Khufu was a ruthless warrior who took over large amounts of land.

FACT

Khufu was also known by the name Cheops. Sometimes the Great Pyramid is called "The Pyramid of Cheops."

What Is the Sphinx?

Anyone who stares out at the pyramids is sure to see the Great Sphinx. The Great Sphinx has stood the test of time. This stone guardian of Giza is one part human, one part lion.

The Sphinx is a huge monument located near the Great Pyramid. The Sphinx has the body of a lion and the head of a pharaoh. The Sphinx is not a pyramid. Instead it guards the pyramid of Khafre, the son of Khufu. Historians believe the Sphinx represents the head of Khafre and the body of a lion. They think builders designed the Sphinx to protect Khafre in the afterlife.

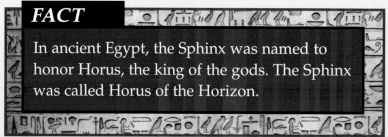

FACT

In ancient Egypt, the Sphinx was named to honor Horus, the king of the gods. The Sphinx was called Horus of the Horizon.

Historians believe the Sphinx is the biggest stone sculpture from Egypt's Old Kingdom time period. It is made entirely of sandstone. Wind, smog, and sand have slowly damaged the monument. The nose on the face has disappeared, as has a small beard. Much of the Sphinx was once buried in the sand. Historians believe the sand may have saved the structure. In 1817 a series of digs began slowly uncovering the Sphinx in the sand.

A carved stone monument rests between the paws of the Sphinx. Builders added the monument about 1,000 years after the Sphinx was carved. The monument tells the tale of Prince Tuthmosis IV. In a dream, the Sphinx told Tuthmosis he would be king. The Sphinx then asked the prince to clear sand that had buried the Sphinx. Tuthmosis became king. He honored the dream and eventually cleared some sand from the Sphinx.

More than One Sphinx

The Sphinx of Giza is the most famous sphinx in Egypt. But it is not the only sphinx in the country. Many pharaohs encouraged the development of sphinxes. They likely used their sphinxes as guardians of a variety of memorials. There are 90 small sphinxes guarding the temples of Karnak at Luxor.

What Is the Red Pyramid?

Red Pyramid

Style: first cased-style pyramid
Date: 2630 BC
Location: Dashur
Purpose: tomb of Pharaoh Snefru
(or Snofru)

Historians believe the Red Pyramid was the first pyramid to have four smooth walls. This pyramid rises 345 feet (105 m), making it the fourth-tallest Egyptian pyramid. Egyptians spent between 10 and 17 years constructing this memorial. It was the first true cased pyramid in ancient Egypt. Its outer walls were once protected by limestone.

The structure gets its colorful name from the red sandstone core under the limestone casing. Later Egyptians took the limestone to make other buildings. This caused the red core to emerge over time. The Red Pyramid shows that a broader base and a lower slope help pyramids stand better.

Egyptians built the Red Pyramid to honor Pharaoh Snefru. Snefru was the first king of the Fourth Dynasty. He established a wide-scale building program in ancient Egypt. He ordered the construction of several pyramids, including the Red Pyramid and the Bent Pyramid. Snefru's son, Khufu, began construction of the Giza pyramids.

FACT

The Red Pyramid is a hit with tourists. Unlike other pyramids, the Red Pyramid has few travel restrictions. Tourists can walk through many parts of the ancient structure.

Chapter 5

Lasting Symbols

the pyramids of Giza

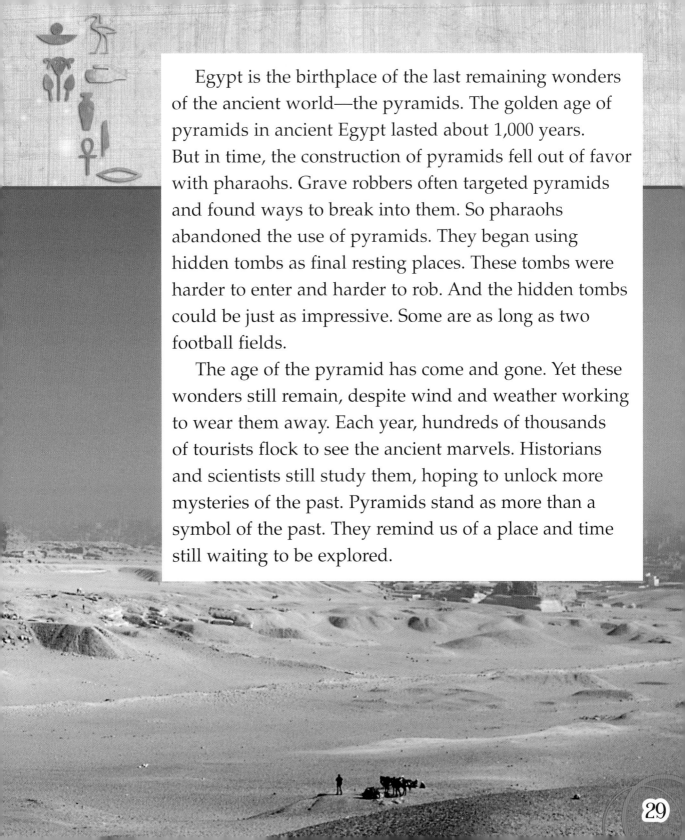

Egypt is the birthplace of the last remaining wonders of the ancient world—the pyramids. The golden age of pyramids in ancient Egypt lasted about 1,000 years. But in time, the construction of pyramids fell out of favor with pharaohs. Grave robbers often targeted pyramids and found ways to break into them. So pharaohs abandoned the use of pyramids. They began using hidden tombs as final resting places. These tombs were harder to enter and harder to rob. And the hidden tombs could be just as impressive. Some are as long as two football fields.

The age of the pyramid has come and gone. Yet these wonders still remain, despite wind and weather working to wear them away. Each year, hundreds of thousands of tourists flock to see the ancient marvels. Historians and scientists still study them, hoping to unlock more mysteries of the past. Pyramids stand as more than a symbol of the past. They remind us of a place and time still waiting to be explored.

afterlife (AF-tur-life)—the life that begins when a person dies

archaeologist (ar-kee-AH-luh-jist)—a scientist who studies how people lived in the past

barge (BARJ)—a large, flat ship used to transport goods

dynasty (DYE-nuh-stee)—a period of time during which a country's rulers all come from one family

Egyptologist (ee-jip-TAH-luh-jist)—a person who studies Egypt

graffiti (gruh-FEE-tee)—pictures or words painted on buildings

hieroglyph (HYE-ruh-glif)—a picture or symbol used in the ancient Egyptian system of writing

mastaba (MAS-tuh-buh)—a rectangular tomb made from mud or stone

pharaoh (FAIR-oh)—a king of ancient Egypt

quarry (KWOR-ee)—a place where stone or other minerals are dug from the ground

sarcophagus (sar-KAH-fuh-guhs)—a stone coffin; the ancient Egyptians placed inner coffins into a sarcophagus

READ MORE

Asselin, Kristine Carlson. *Pharaohs and Dynasties of Ancient Egypt.* Ancient Egyptian Civilization. Mankato, Minn: Capstone Press, 2012.

Riggs, Kate. *Egyptian Pyramids.* Places of Old. Mankato, Minn: Creative Education, 2009.

Weil, Ann. *The World's Most Amazing Pyramids.* Landmark Top Tens. Chicago: Raintree, 2012.

Williams, Brenda, and Brian Williams. *Reach for the Stars: Ancient Egyptian Pyramids.* Fusion. Chicago: Raintree, 2008.

INTERNET SITES

FactHound offers a safe, fun way to find Internet sites related to this book. All of the sites on FactHound have been researched by our staff.

Here's all you do:

Visit *www.facthound.com*

Type in this code: 9781429676328

Super-cool stuff!

Check out projects, games and lots more at
www.capstonekids.com

INDEX